NOTHING BUT THE
BEST

Pictures that capture a legend during his pomp

ON SEPTEMBER 14, 1963, The Beatles went to the top of the singles chart for the second time with *'She Loves You'*. That same day, Manchester United fans first set eyes on another mop-top who would capture the spirit of the Sixties.

George Best, aged 17, was thrown into the United side who took on West Brom at Old Trafford by legendary manager Matt Busby, who knew he had a special talent on his hands.

It wasn't long before his dazzling skill, looks and personality captivated a nation that was in thrall to his style, on and off the pitch.

He became the first pop-star footballer, embracing the trappings of fame that brought wealth, girlfriends, fashionable clothes and fast cars.

However, it's his achievements for Manchester United that ultimately define him and this Daily Mirror souvenir tribute focuses on the peak of his playing career, in the 1960s.

Featuring stunning unseen images recently unearthed from the Mirror archive, we celebrate the most outstanding footballer to be produced by these islands, a man who inspired a magnificent United side to league championship and European Cup glory and thrilled us all as he did so.

Among the 50,453 crowd who saw his debut half a century ago was broadcaster Sir Michael Parkinson, who became a close friend of Best's. In his 2008 autobiography, '*Parky*', he recalled that afternoon:

"Matt [Busby] had told us to watch out for something special but none of us was prepared for what we saw. West Bromwich Albion was the opposition. Graham Williams, a nuggety Welsh international full-back, was marking George. I wrote at the time that Best had the physique of a toothpick, but the heart of a bull terrier. He beat Williams every way up and celebrated his domination by pushing the ball through the full-back's legs, nutmegging him.

"Many years later I was with George when Mr Williams approached. 'Do me a favour, George, and stand still so I can see your face.' George asked why. 'Because all I ever saw of you when we played against you was your a*** disappearing down the touchline'."

Most of the defenders who tried to stop him during the sixties would know the feeling.

Design and production by Trinity Mirror Sport Media

A Mirror publication • Head of Syndication and Licensing: Fergus McKenna • Mirrorpix: David Scripps, Simon Flavin, 020 7293 3858
Trinity Mirror Sport Media Managing Director: Ken Rogers • Senior Editor: Steve Hanrahan • Senior Art Editor: Rick Cooke • Editor: Paul Dove
Compiled and written by: Alan Jewell • Design/ Production: Adam Oldfield • With thanks to Simon Wadsworth
Senior Marketing Manager: Claire Brown • Photography: Mirrorpix, Press Association

ISBN: 9781907324291
Printed by Buxton Press

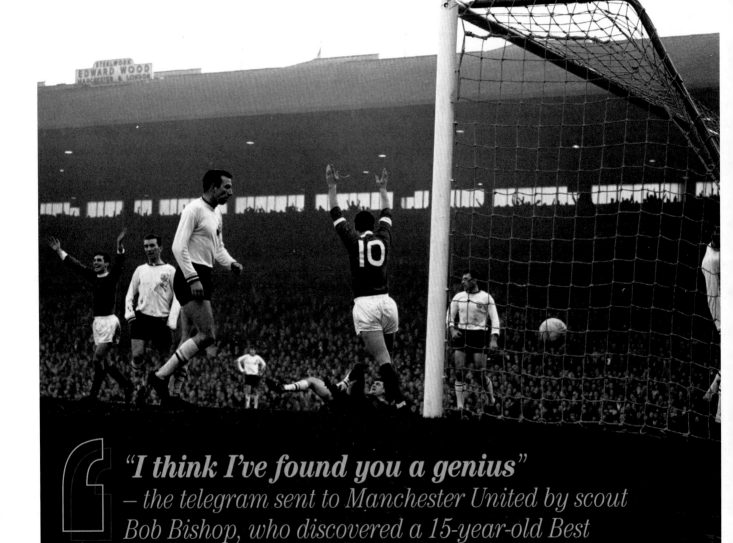

> ["I think I've found you a genius"](#)
> — the telegram sent to Manchester United by scout
> Bob Bishop, who discovered a 15-year-old Best

1

LATE DECEMBER BACK IN '63

The top picture shows celebrations after George Best scored his first goal for Manchester United, in a 5-1 win against Burnley on December 28, 1963. To the left is a United team photo from '63. Best is on the far left of the front row.

2

STREET FOOTBALLER

A couple of young lads have the hopeless task of trying to prise the ball from Best's feet during a kickabout on the road – with not a car in sight – October 1966.

THE **BEST**
50
COLLECTION

3

SHIELDING THE BALL

Once he had possession, the ball became Best's personal property and the opposition would have one hell of a task to get it off him. In this selection of images he maintains control despite the close attention. The image below shows a Division One match against Blackburn in November 1964, which United won 3-0. On the opposite page, he turns his body to keep the ball away from the clutches of a Fulham player.

"He was able to
use either foot
– sometimes he
seemed to have six"
– Sir Matt Busby

4

DIFFERENT BALL GAMES

George was happy to pose for the camera while trying his hand at different sports. In the top image, he plays cricket with some young boys by his digs in Chorlton, with a dustbin used as a wicket, May 5 1968. To the right, he goes bowling at the Top Rank Bowl near Trafford, September 1965, and pitches the first baseball of the season for a Lancashire team, May 1965.

5

FAN CLUB

As Best's fame grew, so did his fan club. Hundreds of letters were sent to him every week and he had to employ a secretary to deal with the volume of correspondence and various requests that came in. Here he is talking on the phone to some excited ladies.

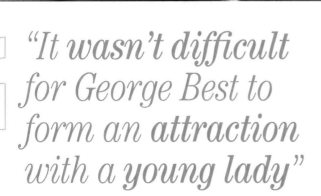

"It wasn't difficult for George Best to form an attraction with a young lady"

— *close friend Eddie Hindle*

6

COTTAGE IN COLOUR

A series of wonderful images from matches at Fulham's Craven Cottage ground. In the main pic, he battles for the ball with George Cohen in September 1964. The top right shot is from March 1967, while the one to the immediate right is from January 1966.

15

'*With feet as sensitive as a pickpocket's hands, his **control of the ball** under the most violent pressure was hypnotic*'
— Hugh McIlvanney

7

TWISTED BLOOD

It was long-time team-mate Paddy Crerand who coined the phrase "twisted blood" to describe what Best's brilliance had caused Chelsea full-back Ken Shellito. In these pictures, he feints and turns inside helpless opponents including West Ham's Bobby Moore (above).

8

FASHION ICON

As well as being the man all aspiring footballers wanted to emulate, Best was a trend-setter in what he wore, having a keen sense of fashion that even extended to opening his own boutiques. The top picture shows him modelling at Manchester Airport, while he is also shown posing at Old Trafford and Tiffany's night club. On the opposite page, he is stood alongside his white Jaguar, sporting a short-lived moustache.

THE **BEST** 50 COLLECTION

More of Best in posing mode, including photos taken in the unlikely setting of a printing office (above), as well as his own fashion boutique (top right and right).

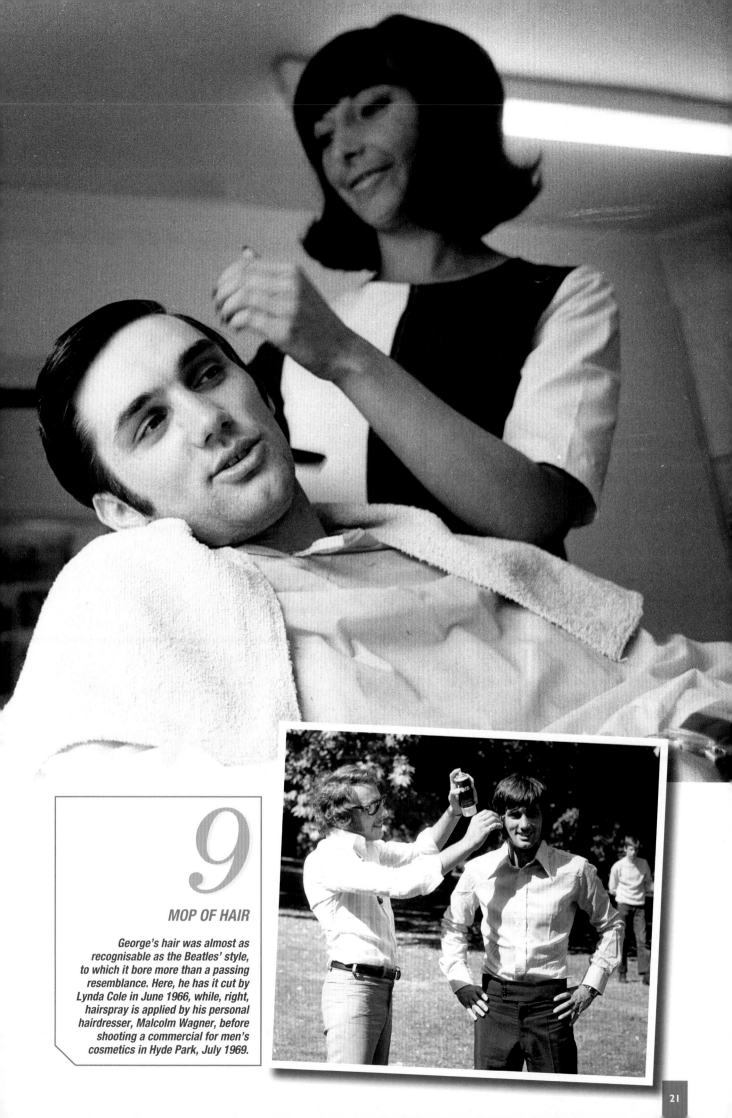

9
MOP OF HAIR

George's hair was almost as recognisable as the Beatles' style, to which it bore more than a passing resemblance. Here, he has it cut by Lynda Cole in June 1966, while, right, hairspray is applied by his personal hairdresser, Malcolm Wagner, before shooting a commercial for men's cosmetics in Hyde Park, July 1969.

*"Manchester United's **glorious history** has been created by people like George Best. Anyone that **witnessed what George could do** on the pitch **wished they could do the same**" – Sir Bobby Charlton*

10

DRESSING ROOM

Inside the inner sanctum of the dressing room, Manchester United players, including Best, Nobby Stiles and Denis Law, celebrate their league championship win with a communal bath (opposite page) in 1965, as well as toasting another title success in 1967 (left). The picture at the top of the page is of Best and David Sadler taking a jubilant shower in the Bernabeu Stadium after overcoming Real Madrid 4-3 on aggregate in the 1968 European Cup semi-final.

11

OUTRAGEOUS SKILL

Best's ability was frequently breathtaking and would leave opponents looking foolish. Here, his back-heel takes the ball away from Tottenham's Phil Beal in a Division One match at White Hart Lane, February 1968.

12

EL BEATLE

The second leg of the 1966 European Cup quarter-final against Benfica was the game where Best really stretched his fame beyond British shores. Still only 19, he destroyed the Portuguese champions, who were unbeaten in 19 European matches at the Stadium of Light, scoring twice in the opening 12 minutes as United won 5-1 in Lisbon for an 8-3 aggregate win. After donning an outsized sombrero following the match, he was memorably dubbed 'El Beatle'. In the Daily Mirror report of the match, Frank McGhee described Best as 'the wilful, skilful waif' who was now 'the young pretender to the "King of European Football" title awarded to Benfica's Eusebio before the match'.

13

CROSSING

There was nothing Best could not do on the football field (he was said to be handy whenever he took the chance to go in goal in training). Although it wasn't his main attribute, he was still a proficient crosser of the ball and created plenty of goals for the likes of David Herd and Brian Kidd. In this picture, he centres the ball during a league match against Leicester City at Old Trafford in August 1967.

More crosses from Best, clockwise; getting the ball across despite a sliding tackle against West Brom in December 1967; a sweet strike at Burnley's Turf Moor during an FA Cup tie in February 1967 and holding the pose against Sheffield Wednesday in November 1966.

14

PINBALL WIZARD

Well before computer and console games captured their attention, amusement arcades provided a source of fun for adolescent boys. In these recently discovered images, George takes a turn at the controls while opening an arcade in Manchester.

"It seems impossible to hurt him. All manner of men have tried to intimidate him. Best merely glides along, riding tackles and brushing giants aside like leaves"
— Manchester City boss Joe Mercer, 1969

15

HARD TACKLES

Football was a much more brutal sport in the 1960s and it was considered a legitimate tactic for the sport's 'hard men' to attempt to take out skilful opponents. No one received rougher treatment than Best but he was more than capable of handling himself and, thankfully, managed to avoid serious injury. On the opposite page, he is shown going to ground against Nottingham Forest in September 1964. In the top picture, he is felled at Bramall Lane on Boxing Day, 1964, while, left, he is upended at QPR's Loftus Road in October 1968. Best is also seen exchanging glances with Chelsea enforcer Ron Harris at Stamford Bridge in November 1967. According to Ken Jones's Daily Mirror report of that match: 'Harris was deservedly booked after two brutal tackles on Best.'

16

DERBY DAY

Then, as now, the Manchester derby was one of the highlights of the football calendar. After their promotion to Division One in 1966, City immediately began challenging their fierce rivals for major honours and Best featured prominently in derby matches from that period. The main picture, above, shows Best striking the ball during the Old Trafford derby of September 1966, while to the left, Best opens the scoring after just 38 seconds in March 1968. The colour images on the opposite page are all from the Maine Road derby of September 1967, which United won 2-1.

THE **BEST 50** COLLECTION

*"It's **something normal** to come back to if you've gone **off the rails** a bit" – Best on his digs*

17

DIGS

Despite the significant money he was earning, Best was happy to continue living in digs for most of his time in Manchester. Mary Fullaway was his landlady at a house in a Chorlton cul-de-sac, complete with privet hedges and daffodils. This was his sanctuary from what became a life less ordinary. He eventually had an ultra-modern house built in 1969 but didn't settle there and returned to Mrs Fullaway three years later. In the image to the right, he is cuddling Mary's grandson, Stephen Fullaway.

18

RUNNING FREE

There were few finer sights in football than George Best sprinting clear of the opposition with the ball at the mesmeric control of his feet. In this picture he is leaving the Burnley defence behind during a 2-2 draw at Old Trafford in September 1967.

More images of Best with the ball at his feet, the main picture above from 1967 and, right, a thrilling dash down the touchline at Highfield Road with the crowd close to the action and Coventry's players in desperate pursuit, March 1968.

19

FIGHTING FOR POSSESSION

Although he was of slender build, Best, blessed with immense depths of courage, was more than happy to mix it physically with those who sought to rob him of the ball. Here he contests possession during the final league fixture of the 1967/68 season, against Sunderland at Old Trafford.

20

STOCKINGED HERO

With less than 10 minutes to go of an FA Cup tie against Burnley in February 1965, Manchester United were 1-0 down. At this point, George Best, who had removed his left boot, took over: With his stockinged foot, he provided the cross for Denis Law's equaliser, before his booted right created Paddy Crerand's winner. He can be seen here shaking hands at the end of the game while carrying his superfluous footwear.

21

FAMILY MAN

Throughout his career, George remained close to his family and can be seen here with his twin sisters Julie and Grace (above), plus mum Anne and dad Dickie, in October 1966. To the left, he poses with his younger siblings again, plus then girlfriend Eva Haraldsted, September 1969.

22

MAN OF THE PEOPLE

Wherever he went, Best attracted large crowds of admirers, desperate for an autograph or simply just to get close to him. He is pictured, right, being surrounded at a bread factory in Stockport, October 1968, plus (top of the opposite page) serving drinks to delighted elderly ladies at Manchester Exhibition Hall, April 1966.

THE BEST 50 COLLECTION

23

WORLDWIDE FAME

George's football ability allowed the lad who once suffered from homesickness to travel all over the world. Here he checks his passport before a round the world trip, May 1967.

24

TRAINING

Before his propensity for late nights and alcohol began to get the better of him later in his career, Best was actually an assiduous trainer. As he said himself: "I knew I had to be fit to avoid being battered by some of the guys who were after me on a Saturday."

The above images show George in his training kit preparing for a Manchester derby in December 1969. Below, he joins team-mates in a session of sit-ups, February 1969.

25
GOLDEN BOY

In the 1960s, virtually everyone wore black boots, unlike the technicolour parade that is modern football. Alan Ball was very much the exception with his white footwear while George was sent these gold-painted boots as a gift in October 1969. If nothing else, they matched his sports car.

Although he was by no means tall, Best was a tremendous header of the ball and scored a fair share of his goals in this manner. Here, he sends a flying header towards goal against Nottingham Forest at Old Trafford, March 1968.

"He had the lot: **balance**, **pace**, two good feet, he was brave, strong and a **good header** of the ball" – Johnny Giles

More classic Best headers captured by camera, including one against Arsenal (above) that was shortlisted in the sports photography category of the 1967 World Press Awards. On the opposite page, he gets airborne at Old Trafford against Leicester City, April 1966, while we see further leaps at Filbert Street in December 1968 (right); an equaliser at Hillsborough, September 1967 (far right); on target against West Ham in January 1968 (below right) and another when Leicester were the opposition (below), August 1967.

27

BEST MATE

Despite the rivalry between their respective clubs, Best struck up a strong friendship with Manchester City's Mike Summerbee. The picture on the opposite page shows George acting, appropriately, as best man at Summerbee's wedding to Tina Schofield in May 1967. Top left, the pair stand at the door of a clothes boutique they opened together, while, above, they leave the pitch after a muddy Manchester derby at Maine Road ended 1-1 in January 1967. We also see Best giving Summerbee a massage at a Manchester sauna, November 1969, and more wedding duties.

Manchester EveningNews

Agenda setting journalism every day.
Meet the team...

Stuart Brennan
Manchester City

Stuart Mathieson
Manchester United

Paul Handler
manchestereveningnews.co.uk
Sports Reporter

Anthony Jepson
Basketball

Neil Barker
Rugby League

Mike Keegan
Sports News

David Ottewell
Sports Data

Chris Ostick
Cricket

Neil Leigh
Sale Sharks

James Robson
Boxing

Peter Spencer
Sports Editor

28

TURNING 21

Best had already been part of two Manchester United title-winning sides by the time he celebrated his 21st birthday in May 1967. In these pictures, he toasts the landmark with mum Anne and dad Dickie.

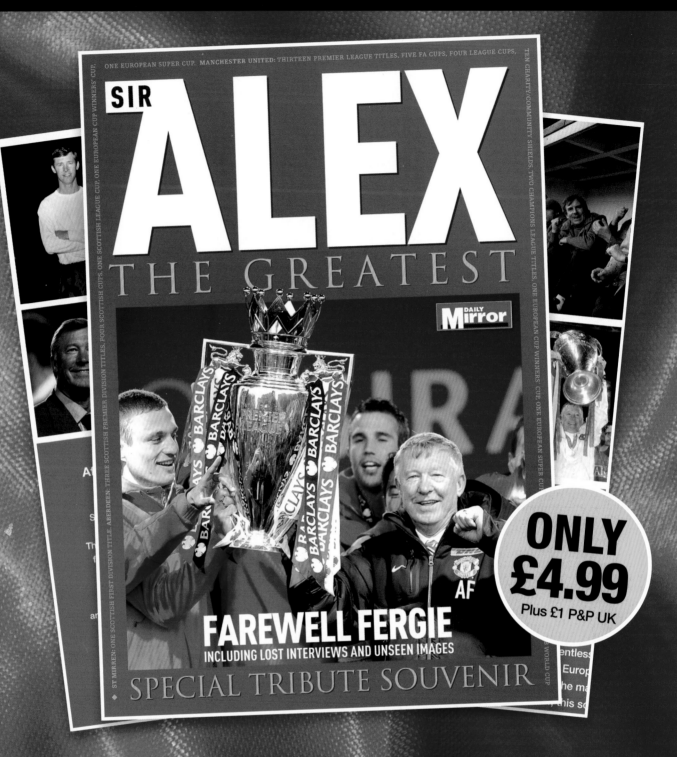

SIR **ALEX**
THE GREATEST

Mirror

ONE EUROPEAN SUPER CUP. MANCHESTER UNITED: THIRTEEN PREMIER LEAGUE TITLES, FIVE FA CUPS, FOUR LEAGUE CUPS,

TEN CHARITY/COMMUNITY SHIELDS, TWO CHAMPIONS LEAGUE TITLES, ONE EUROPEAN CUP WINNERS' CUP, ONE EUROPEAN SUPER CUP,

ST MIRREN: ONE SCOTTISH FIRST DIVISION TITLE. ABERDEEN: THREE SCOTTISH PREMIER DIVISION TITLES, FOUR SCOTTISH CUPS, ONE SCOTTISH LEAGUE CUP, ONE EUROPEAN CUP WINNERS' CUP.

ONLY £4.99
Plus £1 P&P UK

FAREWELL FERGIE
INCLUDING LOST INTERVIEWS AND UNSEEN IMAGES

SPECIAL TRIBUTE SOUVENIR

The lost interviews and unseen images

29

HIS SECOND HOME

Old Trafford was the stage for most of the memorable moments in George Best's career and he also spent plenty of time there when he wasn't playing matches. Amongst this selection, we see him posing with boys who were acting in a film (above), as well as featuring in a United group shot (fifth from the right on the back row) that also included the England cricketer Geoffrey Boycott, who popped over from the other Old Trafford while preparing for an Ashes Test match against Australia.

The main photograph shows George running out behind Denis Law before a league match at Old Trafford in April 1967, while, below left, he poses alongside Nobby Stiles, Bobby Charlton and Italian agent Gigi Peronace.

30

THEY CALL YOU THE BELFAST BOY

The words above were lyrics within the song 'Belfast Boy' by Don Fardon, a homage to the city's greatest sporting hero. In these pictures, we see him visiting Belfast City Hall in June 1968 (top picture) and arriving home for an international against England, April 1969.

31

REAL MADRID, 1968

After the Busby Babes were cruelly cut down in the Munich air disaster of 1958, manager Matt Busby was desperate to build another team that could challenge for the European Cup. Ten years after Munich, the Best-Law-Charlton side faced Real Madrid in the semi-final and it was Best who scored the only goal in the first leg at Old Trafford, which can be seen from three different angles on the opposite page.

"*What he had was **unique**, you can't coach it*"

– Johan Cruyff

Celebrating his goal against Real Madrid in April 1968, which proved decisive after the second leg three weeks later finished 3-3.

32

THE BEST BOUTIQUE

While he was still a teenager, Best went into business, opening a men's fashion boutique in his own name, which was sandwiched between a printers and a betting shop in Sale. Before long he opened another shop, Edwardia, in partnership with Manchester City's Mike Summerbee. In these images, we see him restocking his first shop and overseeing the decoration of the second, which was located on Bridge Street, Manchester.

More pictures from the Best boutique, including him measuring Maxi Turner for a pair of (male) leather trousers to which she had taken a liking. We also see George paying close attention to actress Juliet Mills, who was trying on a toreador jacket, while he poses outside Edwardia with the similarly sharp-suited Mike Summerbee.

33

COMMERCIAL KING

Best's fame, talent and looks opened all kinds of doors to him and companies were desperate for him to promote their products. His advert for Cookstown sausages was probably his most famous endorsement, while here he gives his support to a bread company and a new range of plastic footballs.

34

LIVERPOOL

In the first few seasons of Best's career, Liverpool were Manchester United's main rivals with the clubs winning two league titles apiece between 1964 and 1967. The top right picture shows him scoring from the penalty spot in a 2-2 Old Trafford draw in December 1966, while, right, he battles for possession with Emlyn Hughes in April 1968.

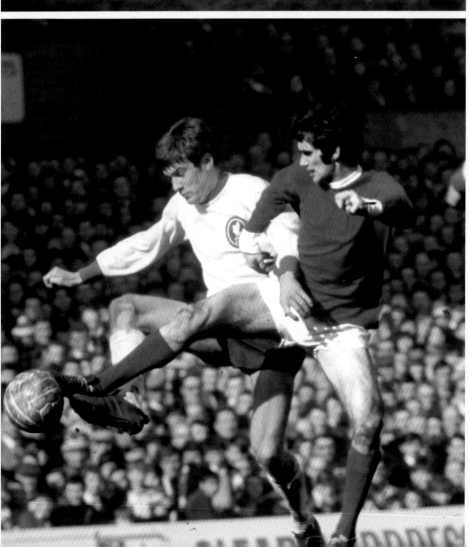

"It was the *finest individual performance* by any player to grace Windsor Park"
— Journalist Malcolm Brodie

35

INTERNATIONAL

Sadly George never graced the stage of a major international tournament as Northern Ireland failed to qualify for a World Cup or European Championship finals during the peak of his playing career. However, he was proud to represent his country on 37 occasions. The picture to the right shows George during a Home International against Scotland in October 1967. So great was his performance, this was dubbed 'the George Best match'.

"If I'd been **born ugly,**
you would never have
heard of *Pele*"

36

GIRLS, GIRLS, GIRLS

George loved the ladies and the feeling was reciprocated. Girlfriends came and went with dizzying regularity, as can be seen on this page. Among the one-time sweethearts pictured here are Jennifer Lowe, Eva Haraldsted, Anne Higson, Jackie Glass and Janet McGregor. There were many more.

THE BEST **50** COLLECTION

37

GOALS, GOALS, GOALS

On 179 occasions in 466 matches for Manchester United, George Best found the back of the net. Hugh McIlvanney, who chronicled Best's career, remembered being present at one of the most memorable, writing the following while profiling Best in 1992: "George Best had come in along the goal line from the corner flag in a blur of intricate deception. Having briskly embarrassed three or four defenders, he drove the ball high into the net with a fierce simplicity that made spectators wonder if the acuteness of the angle had been an optical illusion. 'What was the time of that goal?' asked a young reporter in the Manchester United press box. 'Never mind the time, son,' said an older voice beside him. 'Just write down the date.'"

"*Some people were calling him a playboy; but no playboy was ever more captive to his craft*" – *Arthur Hopcraft, 1968*

A clockwise sequence of another stunning Best goal, which demonstrated his lightning reactions and fierce determination to get to the ball first. This was against Burnley at Turf Moor in February 1968.

*"He was the **finest player** I ever played with or against. I **treasure my memories** of him even though on occasions he made me look rather foolish"* – Pat Jennings

38

NOT THIS TIME

George didn't always get his way on the football field, and there a number of excellent goalkeepers who prevented him adding to his goal tally. Among the stoppers denying him here are Pat Jennings (opposite page), Gordon Banks (above, centre), Gary Sprake (top picture), Jim Montgomery (above right) and Bill Glazier (right).

THE BEST 50 COLLECTION

Tottenham's Pat Jennings resorts to drastic measures to stop Best in a league match at Old Trafford in November 1969. Bobby Charlton fired home from the resulting free-kick as United eventually won 3-1.

*"From 1964 to 1969 **he was the best** player in the country"*
— Denis Law

39

CHAMPAGNE LIFESTYLE

George was quite partial to a glass of bubbly, as these pictures testify. We see him toasting the opening of his Edwardia boutique in September 1967, while keeping two ladies company, and dressing more formally at the Anglo American Sporting club in May 1968.

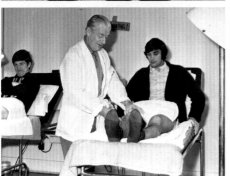

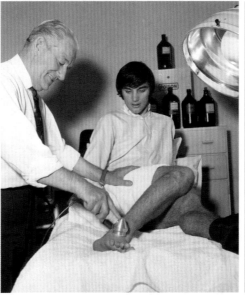

40

MAGIC SPONGE

As has already been documented, football in the 1960s was not for the faint-hearted. George was on the receiving end of plenty of rough treatment, which required interventions and treatment from the physio. Jack Crompton, a former United player, is the trainer seeing to him in the main picture (above).

41

CENTRE OF ATTENTION

Almost every time George Best walked into a room, or onto the football field, he was the main attraction, guaranteed to turn heads. We see him here walking onto the Old Trafford pitch to be greeted by a group of photographers. Top left, he is looking a little over-dressed at the Galleon Pool in Didsbury, June 1966.

42

GOAL CELEBRATIONS

A few images of Best receiving the congratulations of his team-mates – and an adoring boy – after finding the net.

*"His play by late 1967 had developed into the **most exciting individual** contribution to football on view in Europe"* – Arthur Hopcraft, The Football Man, 1968

43

HOLIDAYS

George loved to get away from it all with a break in the sun. These photographs show him having fun in Majorca in September 1967, and receiving plenty of attention from the actress Susan George on the same island, 1969 (right).

44

FLASH CARS

The trappings of fame brought Best a series of sports cars, including a Jaguar and Lotus Europa.

45

CROWNING GLORY

Until 1999 and 'that night in Barcelona' came along, the greatest day in Manchester United's history was undoubtedly the capture of the European Cup against Benfica at Wembley in May 1968. Best scored the second goal as United found the target on three occasions in extra-time to become the first English club to lift the trophy. The top right image shows George evading the Benfica keeper to put United 2-1 up. As the celebration pictures demonstrate, it was a special moment for all involved.

"*I used to dream about **taking the ball round the keeper**, stopping it on the line and then getting on **my hands and knees** and heading it into the net. Against Benfica in the final I nearly did it, **but then chickened out**. I might have **given the boss a heart attack**"*

 "George Best was one of the **most talented players of all time** and probably the best footballer who never made it to a *major world final*" – Franz Beckenbauer

46

SHOWING OFF SILVERWARE

United had plenty to celebrate between 1965 and 1968, winning two league championships and the European Cup. The top three images show the team on the day they received the title trophy in 1967. To the left, Best and Nobby Stiles parade the 'old lady' in 1965. On the opposite page, George and Alex Stepney stare at the European Cup at a pre-season photo call in 1968.

47

FOOTBALLER OF THE YEAR

George became the youngest player to be named the Football Writers' Association player of the year in 1968.

48

BALLON D'OR

An even more prestigious individual award followed when Best was voted winner of the Ballon d'Or (European Footballer of the Year) for 1968. He was presented with the trophy at Old Trafford, watched by manager and team-mates, in April 1969.

49

PORTRAITS OF THE
FOOTBALLING ARTIST

George Best was truly a man apart, as the portrait images that follow demonstrate. This picture was taken at Highbury before a league match against Arsenal in November 1964, when he was just 18.

A selection of pictures of George on his canvas of choice – a football field.

50

CLASSIC MATCH ACTION

We close this special celebratory magazine with a collection of images showing George in his heyday, lighting up the 1960s with his dazzling ability.

From Ken Jones' Daily Mirror report of a United 2-0 victory over Chelsea, published on October 1 1964:

'At the end they stood and acclaimed him. They gave him their hearts because he had won them with every bewitching swerve, every flick of his magic feet. It was that way at Stamford Bridge last night. A night that belonged to a bundle of brilliance called George Best.'

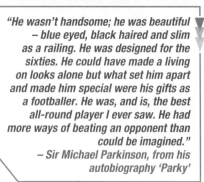

"He wasn't handsome; he was beautiful – blue eyed, black haired and slim as a railing. He was designed for the sixties. He could have made a living on looks alone but what set him apart and made him special were his gifts as a footballer. He was, and is, the best all-round player I ever saw. He had more ways of beating an opponent than could be imagined."
– Sir Michael Parkinson, from his autobiography 'Parky'

"No player before had **captured the public's imagination** off the pitch as well as on it" – John Roberts, George Best's ghost-writer and biographer